Microsoft Excel

The Microsoft 365 Companion Series

Dr. Patrick Jones

OLYMPUS ACADEMY
PRESS

TABLE OF CONTENTS

UNLEASHING THE POWER OF DATA

Imagine having the ability to take raw data and transform it into actionable insights. Whether you're managing budgets, tracking projects, or analyzing trends, Microsoft Excel is the tool that makes it all possible. It's a staple in the professional world, a trusted companion for students, and a go-to resource for anyone who works with numbers and information.

Excel isn't just about rows and columns; it's about uncovering the stories behind the numbers. With its versatile features, from simple calculations to advanced analytics, Excel empowers users to organize, analyze, and visualize data in ways that drive informed decisions and streamline workflows.

Microsoft Excel has been a cornerstone of productivity since its debut. Its enduring popularity stems from its ability to adapt to a wide range of needs, whether you're managing household finances or working on complex business analytics.

Excel's value lies in its flexibility:

- **For Professionals:** It's the ultimate tool for financial modeling, project management, and data reporting.

- **For Students:** Excel simplifies data analysis, making it easier to understand and present information.

- **For Everyone Else:** From planning a personal budget to creating detailed schedules, Excel's applications are endless.

Excel's integration with Microsoft 365 further enhances its capabilities, enabling cloud-based collaboration, seamless sharing, and access to innovative tools like Copilot for generating insights and automating repetitive tasks.

This book is your guide to mastering Microsoft Excel, regardless of your starting point. Whether you're a beginner exploring the basics or an experienced user looking to refine your skills, we'll break down Excel's features in an accessible and engaging way.

Here's what you can expect to learn:

- **What Is Excel?** A foundational understanding of Excel's capabilities and why it's indispensable in today's world.

- **Why Use Excel?** Discover how Excel can simplify complex tasks, enhance productivity, and support decision-making.

- **Getting Started:** Learn to navigate the interface, create workbooks, and perform essential tasks.

- **Best Practices:** Explore strategies for organizing data, building formulas, and ensuring accuracy.

- **Tips and Tricks:** Uncover hidden features and shortcuts to maximize your efficiency.

- **Copilot in Excel:** See how AI-powered tools can automate data analysis and provide valuable insights.

- **Common Pitfalls:** Avoid mistakes that could compromise your data or hinder your workflow.

- **Sarah's Journey:** Follow the story of Sarah as she learns to harness Excel's power to solve real-world challenges.

- **Summary and Reflection:** Recap key takeaways and reflect on how Sarah's experience aligns with your own learning journey.

- **Final Thoughts:** Explore how Excel fits into the larger Microsoft 365 ecosystem and encourage ongoing learning.

Throughout this book, you'll meet Sarah, a relatable professional learning to navigate the world of Microsoft Excel. From her initial struggles with spreadsheets to her triumph in creating a comprehensive data report,

Sarah's journey highlights the transformative power of Excel and the strategies that make it accessible to all.

This book isn't necessarily a how-to guide—it's a narrative journey designed to inspire and educate. Written in a conversational, easy-to-understand style, it demystifies complex concepts and provides practical examples to reinforce your learning.

Whether you're new to Excel or ready to deepen your expertise, this book will empower you to harness the full potential of this indispensable tool. Let's dive in and start your journey toward Excel mastery!

WHAT IS MICROSOFT EXCEL?

Microsoft Excel is more than just a spreadsheet program; it's a versatile, powerful tool that helps you manage, analyze, and visualize data. From organizing simple lists to running complex financial models, Excel provides a structured platform for understanding and utilizing information in ways that drive better decisions and increase productivity.

At its core, Excel is built on a grid of rows and columns, creating a canvas for organizing data. Each individual box within the grid is called a cell, and these cells can hold text, numbers, formulas, or even images. Together, they form worksheets, which are housed within a workbook— a single file containing multiple sheets for better organization.

Key features include:

- **Cells:** Where data lives, each with a unique reference (e.g., A1, B2).

- **Formulas:** Perform calculations and automate tasks using functions like SUM, AVERAGE, and VLOOKUP.

- **Charts and Graphs:** Transform data into visual stories for easier understanding.

- **PivotTables:** Summarize and analyze large data sets with just a few clicks.

Example: Imagine you're planning a budget. In Excel, you can list expenses in one column, income in another, and use formulas to calculate totals, savings, or deficits.

Pro Tip: Familiarize yourself with Excel's grid structure and terminology—it's the foundation of everything you'll do.

Excel's greatest strength lies in its ability to adapt to diverse use cases, making it an essential tool for professionals, students, and individuals alike.

- **For Professionals:** Track expenses, analyze performance metrics, or forecast trends.

- **For Educators and Students:** Organize data for research projects, calculate statistics, or create visual aids for presentations.

- **For Everyday Use:** Plan events, manage household budgets, or create schedules.

Example: Sarah, a team manager, used Excel to track her team's monthly performance metrics. By inputting data into a table and using conditional formatting, she easily identified high-performing areas and those needing improvement.

Excel's Key Features

1. **Data Organization**
   Excel allows you to structure and sort data efficiently. Use tables, filters, and sorting options to make large data sets manageable.

2. **Formulas and Functions**
   Automate calculations with over 400 built-in functions, ranging from basic arithmetic to complex statistical models.

3. **Data Visualization**
   Create charts, graphs, and heatmaps to tell the story behind your data.

4. **Integration with Microsoft 365**
   Excel works seamlessly with other Microsoft 365 apps like Word, Teams, and SharePoint, allowing for smooth data sharing and collaboration.

Example: Sarah combined Excel and Word to create a report that included charts directly linked to her spreadsheet, ensuring updates were automatic and accurate.

Unlike other spreadsheet tools, Excel combines user-friendly design with advanced capabilities. It caters to both beginners and experts, providing a scalable platform for all types of data management and analysis.

Unique Features Include:

- **Conditional Formatting:** Highlight trends or anomalies automatically.

- **Power Query:** Clean and prepare data with minimal effort.

Example: Sarah used Power Query to merge multiple data sources into a single table, saving hours of manual work.

Excel becomes even more powerful when integrated with the Microsoft 365 suite.

- **Teams:** Collaborate on spreadsheets in real-time during meetings.

- **Power BI:** Use Excel data as the foundation for advanced dashboards and analytics.

- **OneDrive and SharePoint:** Save files to the cloud for secure, remote access and version control.

Example: Sarah shared her budget tracking workbook on SharePoint, allowing her team to update their departmental budgets collaboratively.

Pro Tip: Use Excel's cloud integration to ensure your work is accessible and up-to-date anywhere.

One of Excel's greatest strengths is its ability to cater to all levels of expertise:

- **For Beginners:** Start with simple lists, tables, and basic formulas.

- **For Intermediate Users:** Explore charts, conditional formatting, and built-in functions.

- **For Experts:** Dive into advanced tools like PivotTables, Power Query, and VBA scripting.

Example: Sarah started her journey by calculating simple totals with SUM but later expanded her skills to include dynamic charts and automated reports using macros.

Excel is not just a tool; it's a problem-solver, a time-saver, and a data storyteller. Its versatility, scalability, and integration with the Microsoft 365 ecosystem make it indispensable for anyone who works with data.

Now that we've laid the groundwork, it's time to explore why Excel is a must-have tool for managing and analyzing data.

WHY USE MICROSOFT EXCEL?

Microsoft Excel isn't just a spreadsheet tool—it's a game changer. From managing small lists to analyzing massive datasets, Excel offers unparalleled versatility, making it an indispensable resource for professionals, students, and individuals alike. But why should you invest time in learning Excel when other tools exist? The answer lies in its adaptability, depth, and integration with the broader Microsoft 365 ecosystem.

In this chapter, we'll explore the unique benefits of Excel and how it simplifies complex tasks, enhances productivity, and empowers users to make data-driven decisions.

1. Excel Simplifies Data Organization and Management

Why It Matters:
Data is everywhere, and organizing it effectively is critical to making sense of it. Excel's structured grid format and advanced tools help you manage information intuitively and efficiently.

How It Helps:

- **Tables:** Organize data into sortable, filterable tables for quick analysis.

- **Sorting and Filtering:** Find specific information or identify trends with ease.

- **Data Validation:** Ensure accuracy by setting rules for data entry.

Example: Sarah used Excel to organize her team's sales data into a table, adding filters to sort by region and product. This simplified her analysis and saved hours of manual effort.

Pro Tip: Use Excel's freeze panes feature to keep headers visible while scrolling through large datasets.

2. Automate Repetitive Tasks with Formulas and Functions

Why It Matters:
Manual calculations are prone to error and time-consuming. Excel's built-in formulas and functions automate these tasks, ensuring accuracy and efficiency.

How It Helps:

- **Basic Formulas:** Quickly calculate totals, averages, and percentages.

- **Advanced Functions:** Use tools like VLOOKUP, INDEX-MATCH, and IF statements to solve complex problems.

- **Dynamic Arrays:** Automate calculations across multiple cells simultaneously.

Example: Sarah automated her monthly expense tracking by using SUMIF to total expenses by category, reducing her workload significantly.

Pro Tip: Explore Excel's Formula Auditing tools to understand and troubleshoot complex formulas.

3. Transform Data into Visual Insights

Why It Matters:
Numbers on their own can be overwhelming. Excel helps you visualize data, turning raw numbers into charts, graphs, and dashboards that tell a story.

How It Helps:

- **Charts and Graphs:** Create bar charts, pie charts, and scatter plots to illustrate trends.

- **Conditional Formatting:** Highlight key data points or anomalies for quick identification.

- **Slicers and Pivot Charts:** Add interactivity to your reports for more dynamic insights.

Example: Sarah presented her department's quarterly performance using a combination of line charts and heatmaps, making her findings easy to understand and visually impactful.

Pro Tip: Use Excel's Chart Elements menu to customize your visuals for clarity and style.

4. Enhance Collaboration and Accessibility

Why It Matters:
Today's work environment demands seamless collaboration, whether in the office or remotely. Excel, especially when integrated with Microsoft 365, enables real-time teamwork and data sharing.

How It Helps:

- **Co-Authoring:** Work on the same spreadsheet with your team in real-time.

- **Cloud Integration:** Save your files to OneDrive or SharePoint for easy access from any device.

- **Version History:** Track changes and revert to previous versions if needed.

Example: Sarah collaborated with her marketing team on a shared Excel workbook stored in SharePoint. Each member updated their section simultaneously, eliminating version control issues.

Pro Tip: Use Excel's Comments feature to leave notes and feedback for collaborators directly within the workbook.

5. Solve Complex Problems with Advanced Tools

Why It Matters:
When your tasks grow in complexity, Excel scales to meet the challenge.

Its advanced features make it a favorite among analysts, accountants, and project managers.

How It Helps:

- **PivotTables:** Summarize large datasets with drag-and-drop simplicity.
- **Power Query:** Clean and combine data from multiple sources effortlessly.
- **Solver and Data Analysis Toolpak:** Optimize solutions and run statistical analyses.

Example: Sarah used PivotTables to analyze her company's sales performance by product and region, identifying trends that informed their next marketing strategy.

Pro Tip: Explore Power Query to automate data preparation, especially for recurring reports.

6. Integrate with Other Tools for Maximum Efficiency

Why It Matters:
Excel's strength multiplies when used in conjunction with other Microsoft 365 tools.

How It Helps:

- **Power BI:** Visualize Excel data in rich, interactive dashboards.
- **Word and PowerPoint:** Embed Excel charts into documents and presentations.
- **Teams:** Share and collaborate on Excel files directly within a Teams meeting.

Example: Sarah linked an Excel budget sheet to her PowerPoint slides, ensuring that any updates to the numbers automatically reflected in her presentation.

Pro Tip: Use Excel's Publish to Power BI feature for seamless integration with advanced analytics tools.

7. Build Confidence with AI-Powered Features

Why It Matters:
Artificial intelligence takes Excel's capabilities to the next level, making even advanced tasks more accessible.

How It Helps:

- **Copilot in Excel:** Generate insights, automate repetitive tasks, and even build formulas with AI assistance.

- **Ideas in Excel:** Get automated suggestions for data analysis and visualizations.

Example: Sarah used Copilot to generate a dynamic forecast model, saving hours of manual work and impressing her team with its accuracy.

Pro Tip: Test Copilot's capabilities on a small dataset to familiarize yourself with its potential before applying it to larger projects.

8. Excel Is for Everyone

Excel's versatility means it adapts to your needs, whether you're a student managing a project, a business professional analyzing trends, or an individual tracking personal goals.

Example: Sarah's Excel journey started with simple household budgeting. As she became more comfortable, she tackled more complex tasks like automating sales reports and creating interactive dashboards.

Pro Tip: Start small—master basic formulas and tools, then gradually explore more advanced features as your confidence grows.

Microsoft Excel is more than a tool; it's a platform for problem-solving, decision-making, and growth.

GETTING STARTED WITH MICROSOFT EXCEL

Stepping into Microsoft Excel for the first time can feel like entering a world of endless possibilities. Its grid layout, vast array of tools, and countless features may seem overwhelming, but with the right guidance, you'll find it to be intuitive, practical, and incredibly powerful.

This chapter is your first step into that journey. We'll break down the basics, ensuring you feel confident navigating the interface, creating your first workbook, and exploring Excel's foundational features.

1. Navigating the Excel Interface

When you open Excel, you're greeted with its signature grid of rows and columns. This is your workspace, and understanding its layout is the key to getting started.

- **The Ribbon:** Located at the top, the Ribbon organizes Excel's tools into tabs like Home, Insert, Formulas, and Data.

- **Rows and Columns:** Rows are numbered (1, 2, 3, ...), and columns are labeled alphabetically (A, B, C, ...). The intersection of a row and a column is a cell (e.g., A1, B2).

- **Quick Access Toolbar:** Found above the Ribbon, this toolbar provides shortcuts to commonly used actions like Save and Undo.

- **The Formula Bar:** Displays the contents of the selected cell and is where you can enter or edit formulas.

Pro Tip: Hover your mouse over any tool in the Ribbon to see a brief description of its function.

Example: Sarah's first step in Excel was familiarizing herself with the Ribbon. She quickly learned that most of the tools she needed—like sorting and formatting—were grouped under the Home tab.

2. Creating Your First Workbook

Excel organizes files as workbooks, which can contain multiple worksheets. Here's how to get started:

1. **Open Excel:** Choose Blank Workbook from the opening screen.

2. **Name Your Workbook:** Click File > Save As, and give your workbook a meaningful name.

3. **Add Sheets:** By default, a workbook starts with one sheet, but you can add more by clicking the "+" icon at the bottom.

Pro Tip: Use descriptive sheet names (e.g., "Budget," "Sales Data") to keep your workbook organized.

Example: Sarah created a workbook for tracking her team's expenses. She renamed the first sheet "January Budget" and added additional sheets for each subsequent month.

3. Entering Data

At its core, Excel is about working with data. Here's how to start populating your sheets:

- **Click a Cell:** Select the cell where you want to enter data.

- **Type:** Input text, numbers, or dates, and press Enter to move to the next cell.

- **AutoFill:** Use the small square at the bottom-right corner of a selected cell to drag and fill adjacent cells with a series (e.g., days of the week, sequential numbers).

Pro Tip: Use Ctrl + Enter to stay in the same cell after typing, useful when entering long text.

Example: Sarah entered her team's expense categories in column A and corresponding amounts in column B, using AutoFill to extend a list of months across row 1.

4. Formatting Your Data

Well-formatted data is easier to read and interpret. Excel offers a variety of formatting tools:

- **Font Options:** Bold, italicize, or change the font and size of your text.

- **Number Formats:** Format cells as currency, percentages, or dates using the drop-down in the Home tab.

- **Cell Styles:** Apply pre-designed styles to highlight important data.

Pro Tip: Use conditional formatting to automatically highlight cells that meet specific criteria, such as values above a certain threshold.

Example: Sarah formatted her expense amounts as currency and used bold text to emphasize her totals row.

5. Performing Basic Calculations

Excel's real power lies in its ability to automate calculations:

- **Sum:** Add a column or row of numbers with the formula =SUM(A1:A10).

- **Average:** Find the average value using =AVERAGE(B1:B10).

- **Other Basic Functions:** Explore functions like MIN (minimum), MAX (maximum), and COUNT (number of entries).

Pro Tip: Use Excel's AutoSum button in the Home tab to quickly total a column or row.

Example: Sarah used AutoSum to calculate her team's total expenses for the month, reducing errors and saving time.

6. Saving and Sharing Your Work

Once you've created and formatted your workbook, it's time to save and share it:

- **Save to the Cloud:** Save your workbook to OneDrive or SharePoint for easy access from any device.
- **Share:** Click the Share button to invite others to collaborate on your workbook.
- **Export:** Save your file as a PDF if you need to share a read-only version.

Pro Tip: Use Excel's version history to track changes and revert to earlier versions if needed.

Example: Sarah saved her workbook to OneDrive and shared a link with her team, allowing them to review and edit the file collaboratively.

7. Exploring Help and Resources

Excel's Help feature provides instant answers to your questions:

- **Search Bar:** Use the "Tell me what you want to do" bar at the top of the Ribbon for guidance on any feature.
- **Help Tab:** Access tutorials and resources directly within Excel.
- **Online Tutorials:** Explore Microsoft's support site or YouTube for detailed how-to guides.

Pro Tip: Don't hesitate to experiment with features; Excel's Undo button is your safety net.

Example: Sarah used the Help feature to quickly learn how to apply conditional formatting to her data, boosting her confidence with Excel.

Now that you've created your first workbook, you're ready to explore the next level of Excel.

BEST PRACTICES FOR MICROSOFT EXCEL

Microsoft Excel is a powerful tool, but its true potential shines when you apply best practices to organize, analyze, and present your data. Whether you're a novice or an experienced user, following these strategies can make your work more efficient, accurate, and impactful. In this chapter, we'll explore essential best practices to elevate your Excel skills and ensure your spreadsheets are not only functional but also easy to use and understand.

1. Start with a Clear Plan

Why It Matters:
Diving into Excel without a plan can lead to disorganized data and wasted time. A clear structure ensures your workbook is intuitive and effective.

Best Practices:

- Outline the purpose of your workbook.
- Decide what data you need and how it should be organized.
- Create a layout that flows logically, with input data, calculations, and outputs clearly separated.

Example: Sarah planned her budget tracking workbook by dedicating one sheet for raw expenses, another for summaries, and a third for charts. This structure made her data easy to manage and present.

Pro Tip: Use sheet names and labels that reflect their content (e.g., "Q1 Sales" or "Summary Report").

2. Organize Data with Tables

Why It Matters:
Excel tables add functionality to your data, making it easier to sort, filter, and analyze.

Best Practices:

- Convert data ranges into tables using Ctrl + T.

- Use headers for clarity and include filters to enable quick searches.

- Keep tables compact and avoid blank rows or columns within your data.

Example: Sarah transformed her expense log into a table, which allowed her to sort expenses by category and filter by month with just a click.

Pro Tip: Apply Excel's pre-built table styles for consistent formatting and easy readability.

3. Use Formulas and Functions Efficiently

Why It Matters:
Formulas and functions are the backbone of Excel. Learning to use them effectively saves time and reduces errors.

Best Practices:

- Use relative references (e.g., A1) for formulas that will be copied to multiple cells.

- Use absolute references (e.g., A1) for fixed values in calculations.

- Break down complex calculations into smaller steps for easier debugging.

Example: Sarah used =SUM(B2:B10) to total monthly expenses and =AVERAGE(B2:B10) to find the average, helping her spot trends in spending.

Pro Tip: Explore Excel's Formulas tab to discover built-in functions that can simplify your tasks.

4. Ensure Accuracy with Data Validation

Why It Matters:
Errors in data can compromise your results. Data validation ensures your inputs meet specific criteria, improving accuracy.

Best Practices:

- Use drop-down lists for predefined categories.
- Set rules for acceptable values (e.g., dates in a specific range).
- Include error messages to guide users when inputs are invalid.

Example: Sarah added a drop-down list to her category column, ensuring her team entered consistent labels like "Travel" or "Supplies."

Pro Tip: Use conditional formatting alongside data validation to highlight incorrect entries.

5. Leverage Conditional Formatting

Why It Matters:
Conditional formatting brings your data to life, highlighting trends and anomalies visually.

Best Practices:

- Use color scales to show gradients in numeric data (e.g., high-to-low values).
- Highlight duplicates or outliers with built-in formatting rules.
- Keep formatting subtle to avoid overwhelming the spreadsheet.

Example: Sarah applied conditional formatting to her sales data, shading high-performing products in green and low-performing ones in red.

Pro Tip: Combine conditional formatting with PivotTables for powerful, dynamic visual analysis.

6. Maintain a Clean Layout

Why It Matters:
A clean, organized layout makes your workbook easier to read and reduces the risk of errors.

Best Practices:

- Align text and numbers for readability.

- Avoid merging cells, as this can complicate calculations and sorting.

- Use consistent font styles and sizes throughout the workbook.

Example: Sarah ensured her financial summary sheet was easy to read by aligning all currency values to the right and using bold headers for categories.

Pro Tip: Use borders and shading sparingly to separate sections without cluttering the sheet.

7. Document Your Work

Why It Matters:
Clear documentation makes your workbook understandable to others (or your future self).

Best Practices:

- Use comments to explain complex formulas or calculations.

- Add a "Documentation" sheet summarizing the workbook's purpose and structure.

- Include column headers and labels to describe data.

Example: Sarah added comments to key formulas, ensuring her team could understand and update the workbook when needed.

Pro Tip: Use cell notes for brief explanations and the Review tab to manage comments.

8. Save and Back Up Regularly

Why It Matters:
Workbooks can be lost or corrupted without warning. Regular saving and backups protect your work.

Best Practices:

- Save to OneDrive or SharePoint for automatic version control and cloud backups.

- Use descriptive filenames for easy identification.

- Create local backups for critical files.

Example: Sarah saved her workbook to OneDrive, ensuring her team could access the latest version and recover past edits if needed.

Pro Tip: Turn on Excel's AutoSave feature to prevent data loss during unexpected interruptions.

9. Test and Validate Your Work

Why It Matters:
Mistakes can undermine your efforts, but regular testing ensures accuracy and reliability.

Best Practices:

- Cross-check formulas with manual calculations.

- Use small sample datasets to validate complex formulas before applying them to larger data.

- Seek peer review for critical workbooks.

Example: Sarah tested her expense tracking formulas with sample data before rolling them out to her team's live files.

Pro Tip: Use Excel's Evaluate Formula tool to step through calculations and identify errors.

10. Embrace Templates and Advanced Features

Why It Matters:
Excel's built-in templates and advanced tools can save time and elevate your results.

Best Practices:

- Use templates for common tasks like budgets, calendars, or schedules.

- Explore advanced tools like Power Query and PivotTables to handle complex projects.

- Customize templates to suit your needs.

Example: Sarah started with a pre-designed budget template and tailored it to her department's specific categories and reporting style.

Pro Tip: Visit the Microsoft Office template library for inspiration and ready-to-use designs.

By following these best practices, you'll create Excel workbooks that are efficient, accurate, and visually appealing.

TIPS AND TRICKS FOR MICROSOFT EXCEL

Microsoft Excel is packed with features designed to make your work faster, easier, and more efficient. However, many users barely scratch the surface of what this tool can do. This chapter will uncover some of the most useful tips and tricks to help you streamline your workflow, reduce errors, and unlock Excel's full potential.

From keyboard shortcuts to hidden features, these tips will empower you to work smarter, not harder.

1. Leverage Flash Fill for Pattern Recognition

Why It's Helpful:
Flash Fill automatically fills in data by recognizing patterns based on your input.

How to Use It:

- Enter an example of the desired format in a column adjacent to your data.

- Go to Data > Flash Fill.

Example: Sarah had a column of email addresses and needed the usernames. By typing the first username and using Flash Fill, Excel populated the rest of the column instantly.

Pro Tip: Use Flash Fill for tasks like splitting names, formatting phone numbers, or extracting specific text.

2. Master AutoFill for Repetitive Tasks

Why It's Helpful:
AutoFill lets you quickly populate cells with patterns or sequences.

How to Use It:

- Enter the start of a sequence (e.g., "1, 2" or "Monday, Tuesday").

- Select the range and drag the fill handle (the small square in the bottom-right corner of a cell).

Example: Sarah used AutoFill to generate a series of dates for her project timeline, saving herself from manually entering them one by one.

Pro Tip: Double-click the fill handle to auto-populate a column down to the end of adjacent data.

3. Take Advantage of Conditional Formatting

Why It's Helpful:
Conditional formatting allows you to highlight data that meets specific criteria, making trends and outliers easy to spot.

How to Use It:

- Select a range of cells.

- Go to Home > Conditional Formatting and choose a rule (e.g., "Highlight Cells Greater Than").

Example: Sarah applied conditional formatting to her sales data, highlighting values above her team's target in green and those below in red.

Pro Tip: Combine multiple rules to create a visually dynamic and informative sheet.

4. Use Named Ranges for Simplicity

Why It's Helpful:
Named ranges allow you to refer to specific cells or ranges with meaningful names instead of cell references.

How to Use It:

- Select a range, then go to Formulas > Define Name.

- Use the name in formulas (e.g., =SUM(SalesData) instead of =SUM(A1:A10)).

Example: Sarah named her team's monthly sales range "MonthlySales" and used it in multiple formulas, making her calculations easier to understand.

Pro Tip: Use the Name Manager (Formulas > Name Manager) to edit or delete named ranges as needed.

5. Explore the Power of PivotTables

Why It's Helpful:
PivotTables allow you to summarize and analyze large datasets quickly.

How to Use It:

- Select your data range and go to Insert > PivotTable.

- Drag and drop fields into the Rows, Columns, and Values areas to structure your analysis.

Example: Sarah used a PivotTable to analyze sales data by region, product, and quarter, creating a dynamic report in minutes.

Pro Tip: Experiment with PivotCharts to visualize your PivotTable data instantly.

6. Simplify Data Entry with Drop-Down Lists

Why It's Helpful:
Drop-down lists reduce errors and standardize data entry.

How to Use It:

- Go to Data > Data Validation.

- Select "List" and specify the items for the drop-down.

Example: Sarah added a drop-down list of expense categories to ensure her team entered consistent labels like "Travel" or "Supplies."

Pro Tip: Use a named range to dynamically update the drop-down list as new options are added.

7. Use Excel's "Ideas" Feature for Insights

Why It's Helpful:
The "Ideas" tool provides automated suggestions for visualizations and trends in your data.

How to Use It:

- Highlight your data range and go to Home > Ideas.

- Explore suggested charts, summaries, and insights.

Example: Sarah used Ideas to identify a sales trend she hadn't noticed, which became a key point in her team's strategy meeting.

Pro Tip: Use Ideas as a starting point, then customize the insights to fit your specific needs.

8. Collaborate Effectively with Shared Workbooks

Why It's Helpful:
Excel's cloud integration with OneDrive and SharePoint allows for seamless collaboration on shared workbooks.

How to Use It:

- Save your workbook to OneDrive or SharePoint.

- Use the Share button to invite collaborators.

Example: Sarah worked with her marketing team on a shared Excel file, tracking campaign budgets in real-time during a meeting.

Pro Tip: Enable version history to track changes and restore earlier versions if needed.

With these tips and tricks, you're well on your way to becoming an Excel power user. Each feature and shortcut builds upon your foundation, enabling you to work more efficiently and effectively.

YOUR AI-DRIVEN DATA ASSISTANT

Imagine having a personal assistant for Excel—one that helps you automate repetitive tasks, generate insights, and simplify complex processes. That's exactly what Copilot in Microsoft Excel delivers. Powered by artificial intelligence, Copilot enhances the way you work with data, making your spreadsheets smarter, faster, and more intuitive.

In this chapter, we'll dive into the many ways Copilot transforms Excel, from generating formulas to uncovering trends and creating dynamic visualizations. Whether you're a beginner or a seasoned Excel user, Copilot empowers you to achieve more with less effort.

Copilot is an AI-powered feature integrated into Excel that acts as your virtual assistant. It works alongside you, understanding natural language prompts to perform a wide range of tasks. Instead of manually creating formulas, analyzing data, or designing charts, you can simply tell Copilot what you need, and it will handle the rest.

Key Capabilities Include:

- Automating complex calculations.
- Generating advanced charts and summaries.
- Highlighting trends and patterns in large datasets.
- Assisting with data cleaning and preparation.

Example: Sarah used Copilot to create a forecast model for her company's quarterly sales. By typing, "Show me a sales forecast for the next six months," Copilot generated a predictive analysis in seconds.

Pro Tip: Think of Copilot as a collaborator—provide clear and specific prompts for the best results.

How Copilot Enhances Your Workflow

1. Simplifying Formula Creation

What It Does:
Copilot helps you build formulas by translating natural language into Excel syntax.

How It Helps:

- Reduces errors by eliminating the need to manually write complex formulas.

- Accelerates tasks like combining data or performing multi-step calculations.

Example: Sarah needed to calculate the average sales per product category. Instead of writing the formula herself, she typed, "What's the average sales for each category?" Copilot created the appropriate formula and applied it to her data.

Pro Tip: Review Copilot-generated formulas to understand the logic behind them and build your own skills.

2. Analyzing Data for Trends and Insights

What It Does:
Copilot scans your data to identify patterns, correlations, and outliers, presenting insights in an easy-to-understand format.

How It Helps:

- Saves time by automating exploratory data analysis.

- Highlights key findings you might overlook.

Example: Sarah uploaded her sales data and asked Copilot, "What trends do you see in quarterly sales?" It generated a summary noting that sales peaked in Q2 and highlighted regions with significant growth.

Pro Tip: Use Copilot's insights as a starting point, then dive deeper into the data to validate findings.

3. Creating Visualizations with Ease

What It Does:
Copilot designs charts and graphs based on your data and desired outcomes.

How It Helps:

- Automatically chooses the best chart type for your data.

- Provides customizable options to refine the visual presentation.

Example: Sarah asked Copilot, "Create a bar chart comparing sales by region," and it instantly generated a clear, professional-looking chart.

Pro Tip: Specify the chart style or additional elements, such as trendlines or data labels, for a polished result.

4. Cleaning and Preparing Data

What It Does:
Data preparation often involves tedious tasks like removing duplicates, standardizing formats, or filling in missing values. Copilot automates these processes.

How It Helps:

- Cleans large datasets quickly and accurately.

- Ensures data consistency for reliable analysis.

Example: Sarah imported customer feedback data from multiple sources. Copilot helped her standardize date formats, remove duplicate entries, and fill gaps in missing responses.

Pro Tip: Use Copilot's data-cleaning suggestions to ensure your dataset is analysis-ready.

5. Generating Advanced Reports

What It Does:
Copilot compiles summaries, insights, and visuals into cohesive reports.

How It Helps:

- Automates the report creation process, saving hours of manual work.

- Ensures reports are well-structured and visually appealing.

Example: Sarah asked Copilot to "Create a monthly sales report with charts and a summary paragraph," and it generated a polished document ready for presentation.

Pro Tip: Review and personalize Copilot-generated reports to align with your specific messaging and audience.

6. Assisting with Forecasting and Scenario Analysis

What It Does:
Copilot uses predictive algorithms to create forecasts and evaluate different scenarios.

How It Helps:

- Provides data-driven predictions for planning and decision-making.

- Simulates potential outcomes based on variable changes.

Example: Sarah asked Copilot, "What would happen if we increased advertising by 15% next quarter?" It provided a scenario analysis showing potential sales growth based on historical data.

Pro Tip: Use forecasting tools in combination with PivotTables or Power BI for deeper analysis.

Best Practices for Using Copilot

- **Be Specific:** Provide clear instructions for the most accurate results (e.g., "Create a line chart of monthly sales over the past year").

- **Iterate:** Review Copilot's outputs and refine your prompts to improve results.

- **Learn from Copilot:** Use it as a learning tool by examining the formulas, charts, or summaries it creates.

Pro Tip: Combine Copilot with other Excel features like Conditional Formatting or Power Query to enhance your workflow even further.

Copilot in Excel is more than a convenience—it's a productivity game-changer. By automating repetitive tasks, generating insights, and assisting with complex analyses, it empowers you to focus on strategic thinking and decision-making.

COMMON PITFALLS AND HOW TO AVOID THEM

Excel is a powerful tool, but even seasoned users can stumble into common pitfalls that lead to inefficiencies, errors, or frustration. Recognizing these challenges and learning how to address them will ensure you make the most of Excel's capabilities while maintaining accuracy and professionalism.

In this chapter, we'll highlight the most frequent Excel mistakes and provide actionable strategies to avoid them.

1. Overloading a Single Workbook with Too Much Data

The Pitfall:
Placing excessive data in one workbook can make it slow to load, harder to navigate, and prone to errors.

Why It Happens:
Users may try to centralize all their data in a single file for convenience.

How to Avoid It:

- Divide data into multiple workbooks or sheets based on logical categories (e.g., by department or time period).

- Use external links to reference data across workbooks when necessary.

Example: Sarah initially stored all her yearly sales data in one workbook, but navigating it became a nightmare. Splitting it into quarterly workbooks streamlined her analysis.

Pro Tip: Use Power Query to consolidate data from multiple sources without overloading a single workbook.

2. Neglecting to Save Work Regularly

The Pitfall:
Losing unsaved work due to system crashes or accidental closures is a nightmare for any Excel user.

Why It Happens:
Users forget to save manually or rely on auto-save without confirming it's enabled.

How to Avoid It:

- Turn on AutoSave when working with cloud-based files in OneDrive or SharePoint.

Example: Sarah enabled AutoSave for her shared workbook, ensuring that her team's real-time updates were never lost.

Pro Tip: Save incremental versions of critical files (e.g., Budget_v1, Budget_v2) to track changes and create backups.

3. Using Inconsistent Formatting

The Pitfall:
Inconsistent fonts, colors, and cell styles can make workbooks look unprofessional and difficult to interpret.

Why It Happens:
Users apply ad hoc formatting without considering readability or consistency.

How to Avoid It:

- Use pre-defined cell styles from the Home tab.

- Apply themes to ensure uniform formatting across the workbook.

Example: Sarah standardized her workbook's formatting using a professional theme, making her sales report visually cohesive.

Pro Tip: Create a custom template with pre-set formatting for recurring tasks.

4. Hardcoding Data Instead of Using Formulas

The Pitfall:
Manually entering values instead of using formulas increases the risk of errors and makes updates cumbersome.

Why It Happens:
Users may not fully understand Excel's formula capabilities or choose manual input for speed.

How to Avoid It:

- Use formulas like SUM, AVERAGE, or VLOOKUP to calculate values dynamically.

- Reference cells instead of typing numbers directly into formulas.

Example: Instead of typing total sales manually, Sarah used =SUM(B2:B10) to ensure her calculations updated automatically when new data was added.

Pro Tip: Always double-check formulas for accuracy and logic.

5. Ignoring Data Validation

The Pitfall:
Allowing unchecked data entry leads to inconsistencies, typos, and incorrect analysis.

Why It Happens:
Users may overlook Excel's data validation features.

How to Avoid It:

- Use Data Validation to restrict input to specific formats or ranges.

- Add drop-down lists for consistent category labeling.

Example: Sarah added a drop-down menu for expense categories, ensuring her team used predefined terms like "Travel" and "Supplies."

Pro Tip: Pair data validation with conditional formatting to flag incorrect entries automatically.

6. Overcomplicating Formulas

The Pitfall:
Complex formulas with nested functions can be difficult to understand, debug, and maintain.

Why It Happens:
Users attempt to perform too many operations in a single formula.

How to Avoid It:

- Break down complex formulas into smaller, intermediate steps.
- Use helper columns to simplify calculations.

Example: Instead of creating a single, convoluted formula for a discount calculation, Sarah used a helper column to calculate the discount percentage and another to apply it to the sales total.

Pro Tip: Document complex formulas with comments to explain their logic.

7. Forgetting to Lock Cells in Formulas

The Pitfall:
Copying formulas without locking specific cell references (absolute references) leads to unintended errors.

Why It Happens:
Users may not understand when to use $ to lock rows, columns, or both.

How to Avoid It:

- Use $ to create absolute references (e.g., A1).

- Familiarize yourself with mixed references, like $A1 or A$1, for more nuanced control.

Example: Sarah used B1 to lock a tax rate cell in her formula, ensuring it remained consistent across all rows.

Pro Tip: Test formulas after copying to confirm references are correct.

8. Mismanaging Shared Workbooks

The Pitfall:
Collaborators may accidentally overwrite data or create conflicting changes in shared workbooks.

Why It Happens:
Users fail to use collaboration features effectively.

How to Avoid It:

- Save shared workbooks in OneDrive or SharePoint for real-time co-authoring.

- Track changes and use version history to resolve conflicts.

Example: Sarah's team used Excel's Track Changes feature to monitor edits, ensuring accountability and consistency.

Pro Tip: Use permissions to control who can edit or view shared workbooks.

9. Overlooking Accessibility Features

The Pitfall:
Workbooks that aren't accessible exclude users with disabilities and may fail to meet compliance standards.

Why It Happens:
Users may not consider accessibility during design.

How to Avoid It:

- Use Excel's Accessibility Checker to identify issues.

- Ensure sufficient color contrast and add alt text to images.

Example: Sarah added alt text to her charts and used high-contrast colors, making her presentation accessible to all team members.

Pro Tip: Stick to simple layouts and avoid overly complex visuals for better accessibility.

10. Skipping Quality Checks

The Pitfall:
Errors in formulas, formatting, or data can compromise the integrity of your workbook.

Why It Happens:
Users rush to complete tasks without verifying their work.

How to Avoid It:

- Use Error Checking to identify and resolve formula issues.

- Review your workbook with a colleague for a fresh perspective.

Example: Before submitting her financial report, Sarah used Excel's Evaluate Formula tool to verify her calculations were accurate.

Pro Tip: Set aside time for a final review to ensure your workbook is polished and error-free.

By recognizing and avoiding these common pitfalls, you can create Excel workbooks that are efficient, accurate, and professional.

SARAH'S JOURNEY WITH MICROSOFT EXCEL

The morning sun streamed through the office windows as Sarah opened her laptop, staring at a sea of raw data her manager had just emailed her. It was her first big assignment since joining the company: analyzing monthly sales figures and creating a report for the leadership team. The task seemed overwhelming, and the spreadsheet looked more like a jigsaw puzzle than an organized dataset.

Her manager's instructions echoed in her mind: "Keep it clear, accurate, and insightful. No pressure, right?"

Sarah took a deep breath and opened Microsoft Excel. She began by sorting the data manually, dragging columns and rows to where she thought they belonged. After half an hour of work, she realized her approach wasn't sustainable. Errors crept in, and the sheer volume of data made her head spin.

"Okay, Excel," she muttered. "Show me what you've got."

Sarah remembered a webinar she'd attended on Excel basics. The instructor had stressed the importance of organizing data into tables. Following that advice, she highlighted the dataset and created a table. Instantly, the data looked more manageable, with filters appearing at the top of each column.

"Why didn't I do this sooner?" she thought, already feeling more in control.

As Sarah worked, she realized she needed to calculate total sales for each region. Manually adding the numbers wasn't an option. She clicked into an empty cell and typed =SUM(, highlighting the range she needed. Excel calculated the total in seconds.

"Wow," she whispered. "That was easy."

Encouraged, Sarah explored more functions. She used AVERAGE to find the mean sales per product and COUNT to determine the number of transactions. Excel's Formula Bar became her best friend, guiding her through each step.

But it wasn't all smooth sailing. She accidentally copied a formula across multiple rows without locking the cell references. Her totals didn't make sense, and frustration mounted. A quick search taught her about absolute references (A1), and soon her calculations were back on track.

The next challenge was presenting the data in a way the leadership team could understand. Rows of numbers wouldn't cut it. Sarah decided to create charts to visualize the trends.

Using Excel's Insert Chart feature, she added a bar chart to compare regional sales and a line graph to show monthly trends. But something was missing—the charts looked generic and didn't emphasize key insights.

That's when she discovered Excel's Chart Elements menu. She added titles, data labels, and trendlines, transforming her charts into clear, compelling visuals.

Her favorite moment came when she used conditional formatting to highlight her highest-performing products in green and her lowest in red. "This is going to make a big impact," she thought, smiling.

With most of her work complete, Sarah decided to test Excel's new Copilot feature. She typed, "Summarize the top three sales trends from this data," and watched in awe as Copilot generated a concise summary, complete with recommendations for the next quarter.

"Can you create a PivotTable for regional sales?" she asked Copilot next. In moments, a clean, interactive PivotTable appeared on her screen.

As a final touch, Sarah used Copilot to format her report. "Make the header bold and add a professional theme," she instructed, and Copilot delivered exactly what she needed.

"This feels like cheating," Sarah joked, but deep down, she knew Copilot had saved her hours of work and elevated the quality of her report.

When presentation day arrived, Sarah felt nervous but prepared. Armed with her Excel workbook and polished visuals, she walked into the meeting room. As she explained the trends, her audience nodded in agreement, impressed by the clarity and depth of her analysis.

"This is exactly what we needed," her manager said. "Great work, Sarah."

Her confidence soared. She had turned a daunting task into a professional success, and Excel had been her ally every step of the way.

Sarah's story is a testament to the transformative power of Excel. Like her, you might start with uncertainty, but with practice and exploration, you'll uncover tools and techniques that make your work easier and more impactful.

What challenges are you ready to tackle with Excel? The journey is yours to take, and the possibilities are endless.

EXCEL'S LESSONS AND SARAH'S JOURNEY

Microsoft Excel is more than just a tool—it's a bridge between raw data and actionable insights. Over the course of this book, we've explored its powerful features, learned best practices, and uncovered tips to make working with Excel efficient and enjoyable. Sarah's story exemplifies how mastering Excel can transform daunting tasks into opportunities for growth and success.

In this chapter, we'll summarize the key lessons from the book and reflect on how Sarah's journey parallels your own as you develop your Excel skills.

Summary of Key Takeaways

1. **Understanding Excel's Role**
   Excel isn't just for number crunching—it's a versatile platform for organizing, analyzing, and visualizing data. Whether you're a beginner or an advanced user, its tools scale to meet your needs.

2. **Why Excel Matters**
   Excel saves time, improves accuracy, and enhances productivity across personal, academic, and professional tasks. Its integration with other Microsoft 365 tools makes it indispensable in today's collaborative environment.

3. **Getting Started and Building Confidence**
   Learning the basics—like navigating the interface, creating workbooks, and using formulas—lays the foundation for more advanced techniques. Starting with simple tasks and gradually exploring Excel's features ensures steady progress.

4. **Best Practices**
   Strategies like organizing data into tables, using consistent

formatting, and leveraging conditional formatting make your workbooks clear, professional, and effective.

5. **Tips and Tricks**
   Shortcuts, automation tools like Flash Fill, and features like PivotTables and charts help you work smarter, not harder.

6. **The Power of Copilot**
   Excel's AI-powered Copilot enhances productivity by automating repetitive tasks, analyzing data, and generating insights. It's a game changer for both novice and experienced users.

7. **Avoiding Common Pitfalls**
   By recognizing and addressing frequent mistakes—such as inconsistent formatting or neglecting to save your work—you can ensure accuracy and maintain professionalism.

Sarah's story demonstrates the transformative potential of Excel. She began her journey feeling overwhelmed and uncertain, facing a seemingly insurmountable task. Her progress mirrored the process outlined in this book: starting with the basics, building on her knowledge, and using advanced tools like Copilot to take her work to the next level.

- **From Uncertainty to Confidence:**
  Sarah's initial hesitation is relatable. Many of us feel unsure when tackling a new tool or challenge. Her willingness to explore Excel's features and learn from mistakes highlights the importance of perseverance and curiosity.

- **Breaking Down Complex Tasks:**
  By organizing her data into tables, using formulas, and creating visuals, Sarah turned complexity into clarity. This approach emphasizes the value of taking small, manageable steps toward larger goals.

- **Leveraging AI for Success:**
  Copilot played a pivotal role in Sarah's success, showcasing how

technology can support creativity and efficiency. Her experience reminds us that tools like Copilot are there to enhance—not replace—our unique skills and insights.

Just as Sarah discovered her potential through Excel, you're now equipped to embark on your own journey of growth. Whether you're using Excel to manage personal finances, analyze business trends, or create compelling presentations, the knowledge and strategies you've gained here are a foundation for success.

Remember:

- Excel is a tool, and mastery comes with practice.
- Challenges are opportunities to learn and improve.
- Technology, like Copilot, is a powerful ally in achieving your goals.

Think about how Excel fits into the broader Microsoft 365 ecosystem. Tools like Teams, SharePoint, and Power BI integrate seamlessly with Excel, opening up even more possibilities for collaboration and analysis.

EXCEL AND BEYOND

As we wrap up this journey through Microsoft Excel, it's clear that this tool is much more than a spreadsheet program—it's a gateway to productivity, organization, and data-driven decision-making. Whether you're a newcomer navigating your first workbook or a seasoned user seeking to refine your skills, Excel offers endless possibilities to grow and achieve.

But this is only the beginning. Excel's true power lies in its ability to work seamlessly with the larger Microsoft 365 ecosystem. By exploring its connections with tools like Teams, Power BI, and SharePoint, you'll unlock even greater potential for collaboration, analysis, and innovation.

Throughout this book, we've delved into the core aspects of Excel: its purpose, its features, and how to use it effectively. You've learned how to organize data, create compelling visualizations, automate processes, and even leverage AI-powered tools like Copilot. These skills are more than just technical know-how—they're stepping stones to personal and professional growth.

Sarah's story reminds us that learning is a journey, not a destination. She began with hesitation and uncertainty, but by exploring Excel's features and applying best practices, she transformed her work and boosted her confidence. Her success mirrors the possibilities awaiting you as you continue to develop your skills.

Excel is a cornerstone of Microsoft 365, but it's most powerful when integrated with other tools.

- Use Teams for real-time collaboration on shared workbooks.
- Leverage Power BI to create dynamic dashboards that visualize Excel data.
- Store and share files securely with OneDrive and SharePoint.

Each of these tools complements Excel, enhancing its capabilities and providing a comprehensive suite for productivity and innovation.

Technology evolves rapidly, and staying ahead requires a commitment to continuous learning. Excel, like all tools, is constantly updated with new features and improvements. By staying curious and proactive, you'll ensure your skills remain sharp and relevant.

The Microsoft 365 Companion Series is here to support your journey. Each book in the series explores a different tool, offering practical insights and strategies to help you thrive in today's digital world. Whether it's PowerPoint, Teams, or SharePoint, there's always more to discover.

As you close this book, consider the opportunities ahead. How will you apply what you've learned to solve problems, streamline workflows, or create something new? What other tools in the Microsoft 365 ecosystem might complement your Excel skills?

Take the lessons from this book into your next project, presentation, or analysis. Share your knowledge with others, explore additional features, and don't be afraid to experiment. Mastery comes with practice, and every spreadsheet you create is a step forward.

Excel is more than just software; it's a partner in your journey toward efficiency and excellence. By understanding its features, embracing its potential, and integrating it with other tools, you can unlock transformative possibilities for yourself and your work.

Thank you for taking this journey through Excel. As you continue exploring the Microsoft 365 ecosystem, remember that the skills you develop here will empower you to tackle challenges, seize opportunities, and achieve your goals.

Here's to your success with Excel and beyond!